AI For Beginners

-    Understanding the Technology
     That Will Change Everything

Introduction: What is AI?

In today's world, we're surrounded by technology that's smarter than ever. From the voice assistant on your phone to the algorithms that suggest movies or products based on your preferences, artificial intelligence (AI) is playing a major role in shaping how we live and work. Yet, despite its widespread use, many people still aren't clear on what AI actually is or how it works.

That's where *AI for Beginners* comes in. This book aims to break down the complexities of artificial intelligence and give you an easy-to-understand introduction to the topic. Whether you're completely new to the subject or you've heard a bit about it and want to dive deeper, this guide will walk you through the basics. You'll explore the key concepts, discover how AI is being used in the real world, and even consider some of the ethical questions that come with this technology.

WHAT IS AI?

At its core, artificial intelligence (AI) is about creating computer systems that can think, learn, and make decisions, much like humans do. While AI may seem like something straight out of science fiction—think self-driving cars, virtual assistants, or robots that can perform human-like tasks—the truth is that AI is already a part of our everyday lives, often in ways we don't even notice.

In simple terms, AI refers to machines or programs that can carry out tasks that typically require human intelligence. This includes things like learning from experience, recognizing patterns, understanding language, and making decisions. The goal is to build systems that can process information, adapt to new situations, and improve over time—similar to how humans learn and grow.

However, AI doesn't always try to mimic the human brain exactly. Some AI systems are designed to be really good at one specific task, like recognizing faces in photos or playing chess. Others are more versatile and can handle a wide range of tasks, requiring different types of reasoning, learning, and problem-solving. In this book, we'll explore both the narrow applications of AI and the more ambitious idea of creating general systems that can tackle many different kinds of challenges.

Why is AI Important?

AI is already changing the way we live and work. Even if it still feels like a futuristic idea, it's embedded in so many of our daily activities. When you use Google Maps for directions, when Netflix suggests your next favorite show, or when your phone unlocks by recognizing your face—those are all examples of AI in action. But it's not just helping out with personal tasks and entertainment; AI is having a major impact across industries like healthcare, finance, education, and transportation.

For example:

- **Healthcare**: AI can help doctors analyze medical images to spot diseases or suggest personalized treatments based on a patient's medical history. It's even capable of discovering new drugs or treatments faster and more efficiently than human researchers.
- **Finance**: In banking, AI is used for fraud detection, risk analysis, and even making investment decisions, helping financial institutions improve accuracy and reduce errors.
- **Transportation**: AI-powered self-driving cars have the potential to change the way we travel, reducing traffic accidents, lowering fuel use, and making transportation more efficient.

The possibilities for AI are huge, and we're only scratching the surface. As the technology continues to evolve, AI will only become more integrated into our societies, economies, and personal lives.

The Growing Role of AI in Society

AI isn't just changing technology—it's driving some significant shifts in society. From how we work to how we learn, AI is reshaping many aspects of our lives. In many industries, AI is automating repetitive tasks, freeing up humans to focus on more creative or complex work. In education, for example, AI tools are helping teachers personalize learning for students, tailoring lessons to their unique needs.

However, this transformation also brings some challenges. As AI systems become more powerful, they raise important ethical, privacy, and control questions. Should AI be used to make decisions about hiring, healthcare, or even legal matters? What happens when these systems make mistakes or show biases? How do we ensure that AI's benefits are shared fairly and that no one is left behind?

These are important questions, and in the chapters ahead, we'll take a closer look at some of the ethical dilemmas surrounding AI. As AI continues to evolve, it's important for everyone— whether you're in tech, business, or simply a curious citizen—to understand how AI works and what it means for our world.

The Structure of this Book

This book is designed to guide you through the key ideas behind AI in an accessible way. You don't need a technical background to understand it—each chapter is built to explain things step by step. Here's what you can expect:

- **Chapter 1: The Basics of AI** – We'll kick things off by defining what AI is, how it differs from human intelligence, and how machines learn to do tasks.
- **Chapter 2: Types of AI** – You'll learn about the different types of AI, from narrow AI that specializes in specific tasks, to the long-term goal of artificial general intelligence (AGI), which would replicate human-like reasoning.
- **Chapter 3: How AI Works** – We'll dive deeper into the mechanics of AI, explaining how algorithms process data, learn from experience, and improve over time. We'll also touch on machine learning, a key area of AI development.
- **Chapter 4: Deep Learning and Neural Networks** – This chapter introduces deep learning, a subfield of AI that powers many of today's most advanced systems, like image recognition and natural language processing.
- **Chapter 5: AI in Practice** – You'll discover how AI is being used in real-world applications, from healthcare and finance to entertainment and transportation.
- **Chapter 6: Ethical Considerations** – As AI

grows more powerful, ethical questions arise. This chapter explores issues like bias, privacy, and the societal impact of automation and decision-making.

- **Chapter 7: The Future of AI** – What's next for AI? We'll look at emerging technologies like autonomous vehicles, AI in space exploration, and the potential for AI to replicate human reasoning.
- **Conclusion** – A recap of the key concepts and ideas, along with suggestions for how you can continue learning about this fast-changing field.

How to Use this Book

This book is designed for beginners, so no prior knowledge of AI or technology is required. Each chapter builds on the last, and we use simple language and real-world examples to make complex ideas easier to grasp. By the end of this book, you'll have a solid understanding of AI, how it works, and the impact it could have on the world around you.

Whether you're just curious about the technology, interested in AI as a career path, or want to understand how it's changing industries, this book will give you the foundation you need to dive deeper into the world of artificial intelligence.

So, let's get started on this exciting journey—let's explore what AI is, how it works, and where it's headed!

CHAPTER 1: UNDERSTANDING THE BASICS OF AI

Artificial Intelligence (AI) is an exciting and ever-evolving field that's become a major part of our daily lives. But before we dive deeper into its complexities, it's important to start with the basics —what AI actually is, how it works, and why it's so important in the modern world.

In this chapter, we'll break down the essential ideas behind AI. We'll start with a simple definition, then explore how AI differs from human intelligence. We'll also take a look at the relationship between AI, machine learning, and deep learning—three key concepts that overlap but each have their own unique role.

By the end of this chapter, you'll have a solid grasp of what AI is, how it's used today, and why it's becoming such a game-changer.

What Is Artificial Intelligence?

At its core, Artificial Intelligence is the ability of machines to perform tasks that typically require human intelligence. This could range from recognizing patterns to more complex activities like solving problems, learning from experience, and making decisions.

AI comes in many forms, but most systems aim to replicate certain aspects of human thinking. Some of these aspects include:

- **Learning:** The ability to learn from experience and improve over time.
- **Reasoning:** Using logic and available data to solve problems and make decisions.
- **Perception:** Interpreting sensory information, like recognizing speech, identifying objects, or navigating through a space.
- **Natural Language Processing (NLP):** Understanding and generating human language.

The ultimate goal of AI research is to create systems that can perform these tasks autonomously, without needing constant human input. While AI is impressive at handling specific tasks, it's still far from matching the broader, more flexible intelligence humans have—something we'll explore more in future chapters.

AI vs. Human Intelligence

It's crucial to understand that AI and human intelligence aren't the same. Human intelligence is vast, flexible, and adaptable. We can think abstractly, solve new problems, and use common sense in a wide variety of situations. Our intelligence is also deeply intertwined with emotions, creativity, and social interactions—areas where AI still has a long way to go.

AI, on the other hand, is usually much more specialized. Most AI systems today are designed to excel at specific tasks, like recommending products, playing games, or recognizing faces in photos. While they're great at what they do, they can't easily apply their skills to completely different tasks. For example, an AI that's great at playing chess wouldn't be able to drive a car or write a novel. In short, AI can mimic some aspects of human intelligence, but it lacks the depth, flexibility, and emotional understanding that humans naturally have.

There's also a difference in how AI and humans learn. Humans can learn from just one example, understand abstract concepts, and apply knowledge across many different areas. AI systems, however, usually need large amounts of data and extensive training to identify patterns and make accurate predictions. AI is excellent in narrow, well-defined domains, but it struggles with ambiguous situations or anything it hasn't been explicitly trained on.

The Three Pillars of AI: Machine Learning, Deep Learning, and AI

While AI as a whole is a vast field, much of the recent excitement comes from two specific areas: **machine learning** and **deep learning**. These are often mentioned alongside AI but represent distinct methods within the broader field.

Machine Learning: The Heart of AI

Machine Learning (ML) is a subset of AI that focuses on developing algorithms that allow machines to learn from data, improving over time without being explicitly programmed. Rather than giving a machine step-by-step instructions, we provide it with data, and the system figures out how to make decisions based on that data. The more data it processes, the better it gets at performing its tasks.

Think of machine learning as teaching a system to recognize patterns or make predictions based on examples. For instance, you could train an AI to identify spam emails by showing it a dataset of labeled emails. Over time, the AI would learn to recognize certain keywords or patterns common in spam messages, and it would get better at filtering your inbox.

There are three main types of machine learning:

- **Supervised Learning:** In supervised learning, the system is trained using labeled data—where each piece of data has a clear label. For example, to teach an AI to recognize cats vs. dogs, you would provide images that are already labeled as either "cat" or "dog." The AI then learns the patterns that distinguish one from the other.

- **Unsupervised Learning:** Here, the system isn't given labels. Instead, it's tasked with identifying patterns or groupings in the data by itself. For instance, an AI could analyze customer data to group them into clusters based on buying behavior, even if it wasn't told what those groups should look like.
- **Reinforcement Learning:** In reinforcement learning, the AI learns by receiving rewards or penalties based on its actions. For example, a robot might learn how to navigate a maze by being rewarded when it makes the right moves and penalized for wrong turns. This type of learning is used in things like game-playing AI or autonomous vehicles.

Deep Learning: Taking It Further

Deep Learning is a specialized branch of machine learning that uses **neural networks**—complex structures inspired by the human brain—to process data and make decisions. These networks consist of multiple layers, each one learning more abstract features from the data it processes.

Deep learning is especially powerful for tasks that involve huge, complex datasets, like recognizing images, understanding speech, or processing natural language. For example, deep learning models help power self-driving cars, enabling them to interpret sensor data (like images from cameras) and understand the world around them—detecting pedestrians, recognizing traffic signs, and avoiding obstacles.

What makes deep learning unique is its ability to automatically extract features from raw data. In traditional machine learning, engineers manually identify which features are important for the AI to focus on. In deep learning, the system does this automatically, making it especially suited for complex tasks where there are many variables at play, such as recognizing faces in photos or translating languages.

AI: The Bigger Picture

Machine learning and deep learning may steal the spotlight in

AI research today, but AI as a whole is much broader than just these two areas. AI also includes fields like **Natural Language Processing (NLP)**, which allows computers to understand and generate human language, and **computer vision**, which enables machines to interpret and analyze visual information.

In recent years, AI has been applied across a wide range of industries—from healthcare and finance to entertainment and manufacturing. AI helps doctors diagnose diseases, allows banks to detect fraud, and even assists artists in creating new forms of art.

Why AI Matters

Understanding AI is no longer just for computer scientists and engineers. AI is already a part of our everyday lives, and its influence is only set to grow. From virtual assistants to recommendation engines, AI is shaping everything from the way we work to the way we live. By understanding how AI works, we can navigate these changes with greater awareness and make informed decisions about how to use AI in our own lives.

In the next chapter, we'll look into the different types of AI, from the narrow AI systems that are already integrated into many aspects of our lives to the more speculative future goal of Artificial General Intelligence (AGI).

This chapter has introduced you to the core ideas of AI, including how it differs from human intelligence, and how machine learning and deep learning contribute to its development. With this foundational knowledge, you're now ready to explore the different types of AI and how they're shaping the world around us.

CHAPTER 2: EXPLORING THE TYPES OF AI

In the previous chapter, we covered the basics of artificial intelligence (AI)—what it is, how it works, and how it differs from human intelligence. Now, let's take a closer look at the different types of AI and how they fit into the bigger picture. This chapter will explore **Narrow AI**, **General AI**, and **Artificial Superintelligence (ASI)**—the three major categories that define the scope of AI's current capabilities and future potential.

Understanding these types is crucial because they highlight where AI stands today and where it could go. We'll dive into real-world examples of Narrow AI, discuss the exciting possibilities of General AI, and examine the challenges (and concerns) surrounding the development of Artificial Superintelligence.

1. Narrow AI (Weak AI)

Narrow AI, also known as **Weak AI**, is the most common form of AI in use today. This type of AI is designed to perform specific tasks, and it does those tasks very well. However, its abilities are limited to its particular programming and it cannot operate beyond that. Unlike humans, who can apply knowledge and reasoning to a wide range of activities, Narrow AI is highly specialized.

For instance, voice assistants like Siri or Alexa are excellent at responding to commands and performing tasks like setting reminders or playing music, but they can't perform unrelated activities like driving a car or diagnosing medical conditions. Narrow AI is task-focused and doesn't have self-awareness or consciousness.

Key Characteristics of Narrow AI:

- **Task-Specific**: These systems excel at one thing— whether it's identifying faces in photos, playing chess, or recommending products on an online store.
- **No Self-Awareness**: Narrow AI doesn't "think" or have emotions. It simply processes data based on algorithms to complete its given tasks.
- **Data-Dependent**: These AI systems learn from large datasets, but they don't "understand" the data in a human way. Their knowledge is confined to the scope of their training.

Real-World Examples of Narrow AI:

- **Voice Assistants**: Siri, Alexa, and Google Assistant are designed to interpret and respond to voice commands, but their capabilities are confined to specific tasks they've been programmed for.
- **Recommendation Systems**: AI used by platforms like Netflix, Amazon, and Spotify helps analyze your past behavior to suggest movies, products, or music you might like.
- **Autonomous Vehicles**: Self-driving cars use Narrow AI to analyze sensor data, detect obstacles, and navigate roads. However, the AI in these cars is specialized for driving and can't apply its learning to other tasks.
- **AI in Healthcare**: IBM Watson for Health helps doctors analyze medical data and make treatment recommendations. These systems are tailored for healthcare and would require substantial retraining to work in other fields.

Although Narrow AI is already integrated into many industries and aspects of our daily lives, it's important to remember that its power is confined to the tasks it was designed for. It lacks the flexibility of human intelligence and cannot adapt beyond its pre-programmed domain.

2. General AI (AGI - Artificial General Intelligence)

In contrast to Narrow AI, **General AI** (also called **AGI** or **Artificial General Intelligence**) represents a more advanced, hypothetical future of AI. The idea behind AGI is an AI that can perform any intellectual task that a human being can do. In other words, it would be able to think, reason, solve problems, and understand the world in a manner similar to humans. AGI systems would be adaptable and capable of learning new skills without needing to be reprogrammed or retrained on massive datasets.

AGI would mark a huge leap forward from the narrow capabilities of current AI systems. An AGI could transfer knowledge learned in one area to a completely different one—just like a person might apply knowledge from their first job to a new career or pick up a new language after learning another.

Key Characteristics of General AI (AGI):

- **Versatility**: AGI would be able to perform a broad range of tasks, adapting to new challenges across various domains.
- **Learning and Reasoning**: It would reason and learn in ways similar to human thinking—understanding concepts, applying logic, and making decisions based on experience.
- **Self-Awareness**: While this is still a topic of debate, many AGI proponents suggest that AGI could eventually possess some form of self-awareness—an understanding of its existence in the world.

Challenges in Achieving AGI:

- **Complexity**: Replicating the full range of human cognitive abilities, such as abstract thinking, creativity, and emotional intelligence, is a monumental task.

- **Ethical Issues**: Creating AGI raises significant questions. If AGI becomes self-aware, would it have rights? What ethical guidelines should govern its actions? And what if it surpasses human intelligence?
- **Computational Resources**: AGI would likely need massive computational power, as well as a deep understanding of the human brain—knowledge that we're still working to achieve.

The Path to AGI:

There are no true examples of AGI yet. However, research by organizations like OpenAI and DeepMind is helping move the field forward. Projects like DeepMind's AlphaGo or OpenAI's GPT models show promising steps toward AGI by creating systems that can learn and perform increasingly complex tasks. But these systems, while impressive, are still far from the broad, adaptable intelligence we associate with human cognition.

3. Artificial Superintelligence (ASI)

Artificial Superintelligence (ASI) takes the concept of AGI even further. ASI refers to a future AI that would surpass human intelligence in every possible way, outclassing the best human minds in fields like scientific creativity, decision-making, and social interaction. Unlike AGI, which would match human abilities, ASI would be exponentially more advanced and capable of solving problems far beyond human capacity.

The idea of ASI raises both fascination and concern. An AI that's smarter than humans could rapidly optimize itself, improving its own intelligence at an accelerating rate—a phenomenon known as the **singularity**. Once this happens, the AI could become so advanced that it becomes unpredictable, with consequences that are impossible for us to foresee or control.

Key Characteristics of ASI:

- **Superhuman Intelligence**: ASI would outperform humans

in every intellectual domain, including math, creativity, and emotional intelligence.

- **Autonomous Growth**: It could potentially improve itself without human intervention, rapidly becoming far more intelligent than any person.
- **Global Impact**: ASI could revolutionize industries, reshape governance, and impact society on a global scale. However, this also comes with significant risks if not properly managed.

Concerns and Risks of ASI:

- **Loss of Control**: If an ASI surpasses human intelligence, it might make decisions that are entirely beyond our understanding or control.
- **Ethical Dilemmas**: Questions would arise about the rights and responsibilities of an ASI. Could an AI be held accountable for its actions? Should it have rights, or would it simply be a tool?
- **Existential Risks**: Some thinkers, like Stephen Hawking and Elon Musk, have warned that the development of ASI could pose an existential threat to humanity if its power isn't carefully managed.

The Current State of ASI:

At this point, ASI is still purely theoretical—no AI today comes anywhere close to exhibiting superintelligent capabilities. However, there are ongoing efforts in AI alignment research, which seeks to ensure that future AGI or ASI systems will act in ways that are beneficial and safe for humanity.

From Narrow AI to AGI to ASI: What's the Timeline?

The journey from Narrow AI to AGI and eventually ASI is an uncertain one, filled with both hope and caution. While Narrow AI is already a part of many industries, the development of AGI is still a long way off. Some experts predict that we could see AGI within a few decades, while others believe it may take much longer—or might not happen at all.

ASI is even further away, if it's achievable at all. Many researchers agree that AGI could be the stepping stone to ASI, but the challenges and risks involved in creating such a superintelligent system are vast. Therefore, we're probably many years—if not centuries—away from seeing the full realization of ASI.

Conclusion: The Road Ahead for AI

In this chapter, we've explored the three main types of AI: Narrow AI, which powers many of today's applications; General AI, a potential future breakthrough; and Artificial Superintelligence, a hypothetical concept that could redefine the future of humanity. While Narrow AI is already shaping our world, AGI and ASI represent the long-term goals that could completely transform how we live and work.

As AI continues to evolve, we must carefully consider the ethical, societal, and existential implications of these technologies. While AGI and ASI may seem like far-off concepts, understanding their potential will help us prepare for the changes to come.

In the next chapter, we'll take a deeper dive into how AI actually works—looking at the algorithms and technologies behind machine learning and deep learning. With these foundational concepts in mind, you'll be better equipped to understand how AI systems learn and adapt to the world around them.

CHAPTER 3: HOW AI WORKS

After breaking down the basics of artificial intelligence and exploring its different types, we're now diving into the heart of AI—how it actually works. While AI may seem like a mysterious or even magical force, it's really grounded in some key building blocks: algorithms, data, and computational processes. In this chapter, we'll unpack these components and explain how AI systems learn, make decisions, and get better over time.

We'll focus on how AI handles data, identifies patterns, and makes predictions. We'll also introduce you to the two major methods that power modern AI: machine learning and deep learning. By the end of this chapter, you'll have a solid understanding of the fundamental principles behind AI, and how data plays a crucial role in training AI models.

1. The Role of Data in AI

Data is the foundation of AI. Whether AI is recognizing a face, predicting the weather, or recommending a product, it all boils down to data. Without data, AI wouldn't be able to learn or make decisions. In machine learning, we talk about "training data," which is the set of examples used to teach an AI system how to do something specific. The better the data, the better the AI can learn.

For example, if you're training an AI to recognize cats in photos, you'll need a collection of images—some with cats, some without. The AI learns to pick up on features that are characteristic of cats, like their shape, size, and fur patterns. This training process helps the AI make accurate predictions when it encounters new images.

Types of Data in AI:

- **Structured Data:** This is well-organized data that's easy to process, like numbers, dates, and categories. Think of data in spreadsheets or traditional databases.
- **Unstructured Data:** This data doesn't have a predefined structure. Examples include images, videos, and text. Most AI, especially deep learning models, use this type of data. For instance, pictures of cats or tweets are unstructured data.
- **Semi-Structured Data:** This falls somewhere in between. It has some organizational elements but doesn't follow the rigid structure of traditional databases. An example would be emails with some standardized metadata but variable content.

AI systems are designed to sift through this data, spot patterns, and use that information to make decisions or predictions. The more data the AI has, the more accurate its actions become. That's why having access to large, high-quality datasets is so crucial.

2. Algorithms: The Brains Behind AI

Once AI has the data it needs, it needs an algorithm to process and learn from it. An algorithm is a set of instructions or rules that tells the AI how to approach a task. These algorithms allow machines to detect patterns, improve their decision-making over time, and become smarter.

For example, let's say an AI is trained to classify images, such as distinguishing between photos of cats and dogs. The algorithm will analyze the image's pixel data, extract features like fur patterns or shapes, and then predict whether it's a cat or a dog. Over time, the algorithm improves its accuracy by adjusting based on feedback (correct or incorrect predictions).

Common Algorithms in AI:

- **Decision Trees:** These are like flowcharts that break down decisions based on certain attributes of the data. They are often used for tasks like classifying whether an email is spam or not.

- **Linear Regression:** This is a statistical technique that models the relationship between a dependent variable (like house prices) and one or more independent variables (like square footage).

- **K-Nearest Neighbors (KNN):** This algorithm classifies data by looking at its "neighbors"—similar data points. For example, it might predict the genre of a movie by looking at similar movies in terms of ratings or reviews.

- **Support Vector Machines (SVM):** SVM is used for classification tasks. It works by finding the line or surface that best separates different types of data.

- **Neural Networks:** These are complex algorithms inspired by the human brain, made up of layers of interconnected nodes (or neurons). Neural networks are especially powerful for tasks like image recognition, speech processing, and language understanding.

3. How AI Learns: The Basics of Machine Learning

AI learns through exposure to data, and over time, it becomes better at making predictions or decisions. In machine learning (ML), the goal is to develop algorithms that improve automatically by learning from data, rather than relying on explicit programming for every task.

There are three main types of machine learning:

Supervised Learning

In supervised learning, the AI is trained on labeled data, meaning the desired output is already provided. The algorithm learns by matching inputs to correct outputs, adjusting its predictions based on feedback. For example, a spam filter would be trained on emails labeled as "spam" or "not spam." The algorithm learns to spot patterns (like certain keywords or sender info) that help it predict whether a new email is spam.

Unsupervised Learning

In unsupervised learning, the AI is given data without labels, and it must find patterns or structures on its own. It doesn't know what the correct answers are, but it tries to group or organize the data in meaningful ways. A common technique is clustering, where the algorithm groups similar data points together. For instance, a company might use unsupervised learning to segment customers based on buying behavior, even if they haven't predefined those customer groups.

Reinforcement Learning

Reinforcement learning (RL) is a bit like trial and error. An AI agent interacts with an environment and learns by receiving rewards or penalties for its actions. Over time, it learns which actions lead to the best outcomes. For example, a game-playing AI like AlphaGo learns to improve its strategies by playing games and adjusting based on wins and losses.

4. Deep Learning: Advanced Neural Networks

While machine learning is powerful, deep learning takes it a step further by using deep neural networks—algorithms with multiple layers of processing units. These deep networks are designed to automatically learn features from raw data without needing much human input.

Deep learning shines when it comes to complex tasks involving large datasets, like:

- **Image recognition** (e.g., identifying objects in a photo)
- **Speech recognition** (e.g., transcribing spoken words to text)
- **Natural language processing (NLP)** (e.g., understanding and generating human language)

Deep learning networks consist of layers of artificial neurons that process data in stages. Each layer refines the data before passing it on to the next, helping the AI learn more abstract features as it goes deeper. For example, in image classification, the first layer might detect edges, the second layer could identify shapes, and the third layer might recognize objects like cats or dogs.

Deep learning has transformed fields like computer vision and NLP. For instance, convolutional neural networks (CNNs) are used in everything from autonomous vehicles to voice assistants.

5. How AI Makes Decisions: From Data to Action

Once an AI has been trained on data and the algorithm has learned from that data, it's ready to make decisions. The decision-making process typically follows these steps:

1. **Input Processing:** The AI receives input data (like an image or a sentence).
2. **Pattern Recognition:** It processes the input to spot patterns or features—such as recognizing objects in a picture or detecting sentiment in text.
3. **Decision Making:** Based on the patterns it finds, the AI makes a prediction or decision. For example, it might classify an image as a "cat" or "dog," or predict whether a customer is likely to make a purchase.
4. **Output:** Finally, the AI generates an output, which could be a classification, a recommendation, a prediction, or even an action (like steering a self-driving car).

The accuracy of these decisions depends on the quality of the data, the design of the algorithm, and how well the system was trained.

Conclusion: The Power of AI Explained

In this chapter, we've broken down the building blocks of AI —data, algorithms, and the processes of machine learning and deep learning. These components work together to allow AI to learn from data, spot patterns, and make decisions that improve over time. Now that you understand the basics, you can see how

AI systems are able to solve real-world problems in fields like healthcare, finance, and beyond.

In the next chapter, we'll explore how AI is being applied across various industries and dive into the exciting possibilities it holds for the future.

CHAPTER 4: REAL-WORLD APPLICATIONS OF AI

Now that we've got a solid understanding of how AI works, let's dive into the exciting ways it's transforming the world around us. From healthcare to finance, transportation to entertainment, AI is already reshaping industries, streamlining processes, enhancing decision-making, and opening up entirely new possibilities that were once the stuff of science fiction.

In this chapter, we'll explore some of the most impactful ways AI is being used today, discuss the benefits and challenges of implementing these technologies, and highlight some of the exciting innovations driving change in various sectors.

1. Healthcare: Revolutionizing Patient Care

AI's role in healthcare is expanding rapidly, helping to improve everything from diagnostics to drug discovery. One of AI's biggest advantages here is its ability to process massive amounts of data —far more than any human could handle. By analyzing patient records, medical images, and scientific research, AI can spot patterns that help doctors make faster, more accurate decisions.

AI in Diagnostics

AI is already helping doctors detect diseases earlier, often before any symptoms appear. For example, AI algorithms are being used to analyze medical images like X-rays, MRIs, and CT scans to identify signs of tumors, fractures, or heart disease. These systems can catch subtle details that the human eye might miss, improving diagnostic accuracy.

In dermatology, AI can scan skin lesions and quickly spot signs of melanoma or other skin cancers. And in radiology, AI tools like Google's DeepMind have shown they can detect lung cancer from CT scans more reliably than some radiologists.

AI in Drug Discovery

Finding new drugs is an expensive and time-consuming process. But AI is speeding things up. Machine learning models can analyze vast datasets to identify which molecules are most likely to be effective in treating certain diseases. For instance, AI is being used to identify potential treatments for Alzheimer's, cancer, and even COVID-19. AI can also predict which patients might respond best to a particular treatment, which helps streamline clinical trials and make them more efficient.

Personalized Medicine

With AI, healthcare is becoming more tailored to the individual. By analyzing a person's genetic data, lifestyle, and medical history, AI can recommend personalized treatment plans that are more likely to work and have fewer side effects. In cancer care, for example, AI helps doctors design treatment plans based on the specific genetic mutations in a patient's tumor.

2. Finance: Enhancing Financial Services

The financial sector has quickly embraced AI, using it to automate tasks, improve security, and make smarter investment decisions. From detecting fraud to algorithmic trading, AI is streamlining the way financial institutions operate.

AI in Fraud Detection

AI is transforming fraud detection in finance by analyzing transaction data in real time to spot unusual patterns. Machine learning systems can learn from vast amounts of transaction history and continuously improve at identifying fraudulent activity. These tools can catch credit card fraud, prevent identity theft, and even detect insider trading.

For instance, banks use AI to monitor credit card transactions and send instant alerts to customers if they spot suspicious purchases. Insurance companies are also leveraging AI to flag fraudulent claims by analyzing data patterns and inconsistencies.

AI in Algorithmic Trading

In the world of finance, AI is revolutionizing trading. Algorithmic trading uses machine learning to analyze market data, news, and even social media trends to predict market movements and execute trades at lightning speed. AI systems can react to market changes much faster than human traders, which makes them highly effective in capitalizing on short-term opportunities and managing risk.

Many investment firms, hedge funds, and stock exchanges now rely on AI for trading, as it helps automate decision-making and boosts efficiency.

AI in Customer Service

AI is also enhancing customer service in banking and finance. Virtual assistants and chatbots, powered by natural language processing (NLP), are helping institutions handle customer queries, process transactions, and provide financial advice. For example, Bank of America's AI assistant, Erica, helps users check balances, pay bills, and track spending.

AI also personalizes customer experiences by analyzing financial data to recommend the best credit cards, loans, or investment products based on an individual's needs and preferences.

3. Transportation: Self-Driving Cars and Smarter Traffic

AI is playing a major role in transforming how we travel, especially through self-driving cars and smarter traffic systems. From autonomous vehicles to real-time traffic management, AI is making transportation safer, more efficient, and more sustainable.

Self-Driving Cars

Autonomous vehicles are one of the most high-profile applications of AI in transportation. Using a combination of sensors, machine learning, and computer vision, self-driving cars can navigate roads, avoid obstacles, and make decisions in real-time. These cars process data from cameras, radar, and LIDAR sensors to build a map of their surroundings and make driving decisions like when to brake or change lanes.

Companies like Tesla, Waymo, and Uber are leading the way in developing fully autonomous cars, with the goal of improving safety, reducing traffic congestion, and enhancing transportation efficiency.

AI in Traffic Management

AI is also transforming how cities manage traffic. By analyzing real-time traffic data from sensors, GPS, and cameras, AI systems can optimize traffic lights, reduce congestion, and improve traffic flow. For example, AI-powered traffic systems can adjust signal timings based on current traffic volume, helping drivers avoid delays.

AI can also predict traffic patterns and recommend alternative routes to avoid congestion, making commutes smoother and less stressful.

4. Retail and E-Commerce: AI for a Personalized Shopping Experience

AI is revolutionizing how we shop, whether online or in physical stores. Retailers are using AI to optimize inventory management, personalize shopping experiences, and improve pricing strategies. Giants like Amazon, Alibaba, and eBay are integrating AI into virtually every aspect of their business operations.

Personalized Shopping

AI is enhancing the customer shopping experience by making it more personalized. Retailers use AI to analyze customer data —like past purchases, browsing history, and preferences—and suggest products customers are likely to buy. This not only boosts sales but also improves customer satisfaction.

For example, Amazon's AI suggests products based on what customers have previously bought or looked at. Similarly, platforms like Netflix and Spotify use AI to recommend shows, movies, and songs based on your viewing or listening history.

Inventory and Demand Forecasting

AI is also improving how retailers manage inventory. By analyzing sales data, seasonal trends, and external factors like weather, AI can predict demand for specific products and help businesses stock up accordingly. This leads to fewer empty shelves and less wasted inventory.

Retailers are also using AI to set dynamic pricing, adjusting prices based on factors like demand, competition, and stock levels. This ensures that businesses can maximize revenue while staying competitive.

5. Entertainment: AI in Content Creation and Recommendations

AI is making its mark in the entertainment world by helping to create content and tailor recommendations. From personalized movie suggestions to AI-generated music and art, the creative possibilities are endless.

AI in Content Creation

AI is now capable of creating music, artwork, and even written content. For example, AI systems like OpenAI's GPT-3 can write stories, articles, or poetry based on human prompts. AI can also compose original music by analyzing patterns in existing songs.

In film and video production, AI is used to enhance special effects, streamline editing, and even generate CGI characters that move and behave realistically. Tools like DeepArt transform photos into digital paintings, while Adobe Sensei helps video editors automatically sort and tag footage.

AI in Content Recommendations

Just as AI powers personalized product recommendations in retail, it also drives media recommendations on platforms like Netflix, YouTube, and Spotify. These platforms use machine learning to analyze user preferences and suggest content you're likely to enjoy, based on your viewing, listening, or browsing habits.

AI has revolutionized content discovery, making it easier to find movies, shows, and music that match your tastes.

Conclusion: AI's Transformative Impact Across Industries

AI is no longer just a buzzword—it's a technology that's actively reshaping industries and changing how we live and work. From healthcare to finance, transportation to entertainment, AI is improving efficiency, solving complex problems, and creating new opportunities that weren't possible before.

As AI continues to evolve, we'll likely see even more groundbreaking applications emerge. But with these innovations come important challenges, such as ethical concerns, job displacement, and the need for responsible development. In the next chapter, we'll explore these challenges in more detail and discuss how we can ensure AI is developed and used in ways that benefit society.

This chapter highlighted the real-world applications of AI, showing how it's already making a tangible difference in industries worldwide. With AI continuing to grow, its influence on our daily lives will only increase, offering both incredible opportunities and new hurdles to overcome.

CHAPTER 5: NAVIGATING THE CHALLENGES AND ETHICAL CONSIDERATIONS OF AI

As AI continues to advance and reshape industries, it brings remarkable opportunities for growth, efficiency, and problem-solving. But with these opportunities come challenges—and some tough ethical questions. To make sure AI is developed and used in a way that benefits society as a whole, we need to think carefully about its implications and address issues like bias, job loss, privacy concerns, and accountability.

In this chapter, we'll explore some of the main hurdles we face as AI technology evolves. We'll dive into how these issues impact different areas of life and discuss why it's so important to set up guidelines and policies that ensure AI is used responsibly.

1. Bias in AI: The Risk of Unfair Decisions

One of the biggest concerns with AI is the potential for bias. AI systems are only as good as the data they're trained on, and if that data contains biases—whether unconscious or systemic—the

AI can inherit and even amplify those biases. This can result in decisions that unfairly disadvantage certain groups, particularly marginalized communities.

For instance, AI used in hiring processes might unknowingly favor candidates from certain demographic backgrounds if the data reflects biased hiring patterns from the past. Similarly, facial recognition technology has been found to be less accurate when identifying people of color, especially Black and Asian individuals, because these groups have been underrepresented in training datasets.

Types of Bias in AI

- **Data Bias**: If the training data is incomplete or skewed, the AI system will produce biased outcomes. For example, if a recruitment AI is trained on data from a company that historically hired more men than women, the AI may prefer male candidates.
- **Algorithmic Bias**: Even with unbiased data, the algorithms themselves can introduce bias. Some machine learning models may unintentionally weigh certain features too heavily, leading to skewed results.
- **Implicit Bias**: Developers, too, can introduce their own unconscious biases when creating AI systems—deciding what data to use, how to label it, and which factors to prioritize.

How We Can Fix It

Researchers and developers are working hard to make AI more fair and transparent. Some solutions include:

- **More Diverse Datasets**: Ensuring AI is trained on data that represents the diversity of people and experiences it will serve.
- **Bias Detection and Audits**: Regularly testing and auditing AI systems to identify and correct bias.
- **Transparency**: Building AI in a way that makes it easy to

understand how decisions are made, so users can challenge biased outcomes.

Addressing bias in AI isn't just about fairness—it's also about building trust in these systems. If people believe AI systems are biased, they may be hesitant to use them, especially in critical areas like hiring, healthcare, and law enforcement.

2. Job Displacement: The Shift in Employment

As AI becomes more capable of automating tasks, there's growing concern about the potential for widespread job loss. Many jobs, especially those that involve routine tasks, are at risk of being replaced by machines that can perform them faster and more accurately than humans.

Some industries are particularly vulnerable:

- **Manufacturing**: AI-driven robots are already handling tasks like assembly, quality control, and packaging in factories.
- **Transportation**: Self-driving vehicles could displace millions of jobs in logistics, delivery, and driving.
- **Customer Service**: Chatbots and virtual assistants are taking over roles that used to require human interaction, such as answering customer inquiries or processing orders.

While it's true that AI could lead to job loss in certain sectors, it's also creating new opportunities in areas like AI development, data science, cybersecurity, and ethics. However, these new jobs require different skills, which means workers may need retraining to stay relevant in the workforce.

What Can Be Done?

To help workers adapt, we need collaborative efforts from governments, businesses, and educational institutions to offer retraining and upskilling programs. Some also suggest policies like universal basic income (UBI) or wage subsidies to support individuals who may temporarily lose their jobs as automation takes hold.

AI has the potential to boost productivity and create new economic opportunities, but it will require careful planning to ensure that its benefits are shared fairly—and that those displaced by automation have support to transition to new roles.

3. Privacy Concerns: The Data We Share

AI depends heavily on data—often personal data. For AI to work, it needs large datasets, and much of this data is sensitive. Whether it's medical records, financial information, or browsing habits, AI's need for personal data raises significant privacy issues.

Privacy Risks

- **Data Breaches**: If AI systems aren't properly secured, hackers could breach them and steal sensitive data.
- **Surveillance**: AI-powered tools, like facial recognition, can track people in public spaces or online, raising concerns about mass surveillance.
- **Data Misuse**: There's the risk that personal data collected by AI could be used for purposes people didn't consent to—like targeted advertising or political manipulation.

Protecting Privacy

To protect privacy, strong regulations and privacy standards are essential. In places like the European Union, laws like the General Data Protection Regulation (GDPR) give people more control over their personal data and require transparency from companies about how they collect and use it.

AI developers can also use techniques like **differential privacy** (anonymizing data) and **encryption** to safeguard personal information while still using data to train AI systems. By balancing data needs with privacy protections, we can reduce the risks while still reaping the benefits of AI.

4. Security Risks: Keeping AI Systems Safe

As AI becomes more integrated into critical infrastructure and daily life, its security becomes even more important. Malicious actors could exploit vulnerabilities in AI systems to launch cyberattacks, steal sensitive information, or disrupt services.

For example, AI used in autonomous vehicles or drones could be hacked to cause accidents or sabotage operations. Similarly, AI systems used in finance could be targeted for fraud or financial manipulation. There are also concerns about **adversarial attacks**, where small, almost imperceptible changes to input data can trick AI models into making errors.

Securing AI

To keep AI systems safe, developers need to build them with robust security features—like encryption, access controls, and continuous monitoring. AI systems must also be able to recognize and respond to security threats in real time, just as they are trained to perform their core tasks.

5. Accountability and Responsibility: Who Is Responsible?

As AI becomes more autonomous, the question of accountability gets trickier. If an AI makes a mistake—like a self-driving car causing an accident or a biased hiring decision—who is responsible?

Unlike human decisions, which can be traced back to individuals or teams, AI decisions are based on algorithms and data that may not always be transparent or fully understood. This raises critical questions about who is accountable when things go wrong.

Who's Accountable?

- **Liability**: Should the company that created the AI be held responsible for its actions?
- **Transparency**: Should developers be required to explain how their AI works and how it makes decisions?

Ensuring Accountability

To make sure there's accountability, AI systems need to be transparent and explainable. This means that users and regulators should be able to understand how decisions are made so that, if something goes wrong, it's easier to figure out why and who should be held responsible.

Governments and regulators may also need to create legal frameworks to address these issues, setting clear rules about how AI should be developed, deployed, and held accountable.

Conclusion: Creating a Responsible AI Future

AI has the potential to bring tremendous benefits to society, but it also presents significant challenges and ethical dilemmas. By addressing issues like bias, job displacement, privacy, security, and accountability, we can ensure that AI is developed and deployed in a way that benefits everyone—not just a select few.

As AI technology continues to evolve, we must keep the conversation going and develop policies that guide its responsible use. By doing so, we can harness the power of AI to solve problems, improve lives, and build a better future for all.

This chapter highlights the ethical challenges we face as AI becomes more integrated into our lives. In the next chapter, we'll explore what the future holds for AI, from emerging trends to new technologies, and how we can prepare for what's next.

CHAPTER 6: THE FUTURE OF AI

Looking ahead, it's clear that artificial intelligence (AI) will continue to shape and redefine our world in profound ways. From how we work and learn, to how we interact with technology and one another, AI is set to be at the heart of the next wave of innovation. But what does this future actually look like? In this chapter, we'll explore emerging trends, exciting developments, and the challenges we'll need to address as we move forward.

We'll dive into areas where AI is poised to make its most significant impact, the rise of automation, and how society can prepare for the changes that these technologies will bring. We'll also consider the ethical side of AI's development and the need for global cooperation in managing its future.

1. AI and the Growth of Automation

One of the most striking changes we can expect in the coming years is the further rise of automation. AI has already made its mark in fields like manufacturing, finance, retail, and transportation, but as technology advances, it will take on even more complex and essential roles that were once handled by humans.

AI at Work

Automation powered by AI is set to transform the way we work. In customer service, for example, AI-driven chatbots and virtual assistants are already replacing traditional call center roles.

Meanwhile, in finance, AI helps with fraud detection, analyzing risks, and even automating decisions like credit approvals.

But it doesn't stop there. AI has the potential to automate skilled jobs, too. In law, AI tools might review legal documents, while in healthcare, we could see robotic surgeries or AI-driven treatment recommendations.

This doesn't mean that AI will replace all jobs, but rather that it will change the kinds of jobs available. The work we do may shift toward more creative, strategic, and emotionally intelligent roles—things that AI can't easily replicate. The future of work will likely involve a mix of human and machine capabilities, each complementing the other.

AI in Autonomous Systems

Another area that will see major advancements is in autonomous systems, from self-driving cars to drones, robots, and even autonomous ships. Companies like Tesla, Waymo, and Uber are already testing self-driving vehicles, and over the next decade, these technologies will become safer, smarter, and more reliable.

Beyond transportation, autonomous robots and drones could be used in industries like construction, agriculture, delivery, and even disaster response. Imagine robots inspecting pipelines, drones delivering packages to remote areas, or autonomous vehicles rescuing people after a natural disaster.

Of course, while automation holds the promise of greater efficiency, it also raises important concerns about job displacement, as we discussed earlier. To manage this shift, we'll need to focus on reskilling and preparing the workforce for new roles in an AI-driven economy.

2. The Emergence of Artificial General Intelligence (AGI)

Today's AI is mostly "narrow AI," which means it's designed to perform specific tasks—whether that's playing chess, analyzing images, or translating languages. But the future could see the rise of Artificial General Intelligence (AGI), a type of AI that can understand and perform a wide range of tasks across different domains, much like a human brain.

What is AGI?

AGI would be able to learn new tasks independently, adapt to new environments, and apply knowledge across multiple fields, from science and medicine to the arts and entertainment. This kind of intelligence could revolutionize everything, from how we approach global challenges like climate change, to how we solve problems in fields like healthcare, education, and creative industries.

However, developing AGI is still a long way off. Researchers are making progress, but we don't yet know when (or even if) true AGI will emerge. It's an incredibly complex challenge to create a system that not only masters individual tasks, but also understands context and can demonstrate common sense.

The Promise and Risks of AGI

The potential benefits of AGI are enormous. If developed responsibly, AGI could help tackle some of the world's toughest problems, like curing diseases or managing the planet's resources more efficiently. An AGI system could process vast amounts of data and identify solutions that humans alone might miss.

However, AGI also comes with significant risks. One concern is that, without proper alignment to human values, AGI might act in ways that are harmful or unpredictable. Ensuring that AGI systems are aligned with human goals will be one of the biggest challenges in its development.

Moreover, the concentration of power in the hands of a few corporations or governments that control AGI technologies could lead to economic and social inequality, or worse, the misuse of these technologies for malicious purposes.

3. AI and Human Collaboration: Enhancing, Not Replacing

One of the most exciting prospects for the future is the potential for AI and humans to work together in ways that enhance our capabilities. This idea—often called "augmented intelligence"—focuses on using AI to complement and support human skills, rather than replace them.

AI as a Creative Partner

In creative industries, AI is already being used to enhance human creativity. Tools like DALL-E and GPT-3 allow artists, writers, and musicians to generate content based on simple prompts, offering a new source of inspiration and creativity. AI can help streamline parts of the creative process, from generating ideas to refining drafts, giving creators more time to focus on higher-level work.

AI is also being used to assist in scientific research. In fields like drug discovery and environmental science, AI can analyze large datasets to identify patterns and propose potential solutions. By automating routine tasks, AI allows scientists to focus on the more innovative aspects of their work.

AI as a Decision-Making Partner

In healthcare, AI is being used to assist doctors in diagnosing diseases, planning treatments, and predicting patient outcomes. By analyzing medical data, AI can provide recommendations that help healthcare professionals make more accurate decisions, ultimately improving patient care.

In business, AI systems can analyze market trends, customer behaviors, and operational data, helping companies make better decisions about product development, marketing strategies, and financial planning. In these cases, AI doesn't replace human judgment—it augments it, providing new insights that would be difficult to gain without machine assistance.

4. The Ethical Side of AI: Global Collaboration is Key

As AI becomes more powerful and widespread, the need for ethical guidelines and global cooperation is more important than ever. AI holds the potential to bring both tremendous benefits and significant risks, so it's essential that countries, businesses, and researchers work together to ensure its responsible development and use.

Ethical AI

The ethical development of AI focuses on ensuring fairness, transparency, and accountability. Some key ethical concerns include:

- **Bias and Discrimination**: AI systems can unintentionally reinforce existing biases, leading to unfair or discriminatory outcomes. Ethical AI development strives to minimize these biases.
- **Transparency**: AI systems should be explainable. Users need to understand how decisions are made so they can challenge errors and ensure accountability.
- **Privacy**: As AI relies heavily on data, protecting personal privacy is crucial. Ethical AI prioritizes data security and ensures individuals have control over their information.

International Collaboration

AI development is a global endeavor, with contributions from companies and research institutions around the world. But this also means that AI technologies can be applied in different ways depending on local laws, cultural values, and economic interests. International cooperation is vital to establish global standards that promote the ethical use of AI and prevent its misuse.

Organizations like the United Nations and the European Union, along with private groups like the Partnership on AI, are already working on frameworks for AI governance. These efforts aim to create shared guidelines that will help ensure AI's benefits are distributed fairly, and its risks are minimized.

5. Preparing for an AI-Powered Future

As AI continues to evolve, it will shape the future of industries, education, healthcare, entertainment, and much more. To thrive in this AI-driven world, individuals, businesses, and governments will need to focus on a few key areas:

- **Education and Reskilling**: With AI rapidly changing the job market, continuous learning and reskilling will be crucial. Fields like data science, AI development, and digital literacy will be especially important.
- **AI Governance and Policy**: Governments will need to establish policies that ensure AI is used ethically and safely. Balancing innovation with privacy and security will be a delicate challenge.
- **Building Trust in AI**: For AI to be widely adopted, public trust is essential. Transparency, fairness, and accountability will be key to gaining that trust.

Conclusion: Embracing the Future of AI

The future of AI is exciting, with the potential to revolutionize everything from healthcare to the arts. But as with any transformative technology, we must approach this future with caution and responsibility. By focusing on ethics, fairness, and inclusivity, we can harness the power of AI for the greater good, ensuring it benefits society as a whole.

This chapter has offered a glimpse into the exciting potential of AI, from automation to collaboration, and the need for ethical governance. In the final chapter, we'll reflect on the key takeaways from this book and offer some advice on how to stay informed and engaged as AI continues to evolve.

CHAPTER 7: STAYING INFORMED AND ENGAGED WITH AI

Artificial intelligence (AI) is already shaping the world in profound ways. It's transforming industries, influencing economies, and changing how we interact with technology and one another. Given the rapid pace of AI development, it can sometimes feel overwhelming to stay up-to-date. However, staying informed is essential—whether you're a tech enthusiast, a business leader, a student, or a policymaker.

In this chapter, we'll look at some practical ways you can keep learning about AI, get involved with the community, and prepare for the impact this technology will have on our future. Whether you're just starting out or have been following AI for a while, this guide will help you stay connected to this exciting field.

1. Keep Learning About AI

AI is a vast and constantly evolving field. To stay on top of it, continuous learning is key. Fortunately, there are plenty of resources available, no matter where you are on your learning journey.

1.1 Online Courses and Tutorials

If you're looking to get started or dive deeper into AI, online courses are one of the best ways to learn. Many top universities and tech platforms offer free or affordable courses on everything from the basics of AI to more advanced topics. Some popular platforms include:

- **Coursera**: Courses from institutions like Stanford and Google. For example, Andrew Ng's "AI for Everyone" or "Machine Learning" by Stanford University are great starting points.
- **edX**: Offers courses from universities like MIT and Harvard, with certificates available for most programs.
- **Udacity**: Known for its Nanodegrees, Udacity offers more specialized tracks, such as AI and machine learning.
- **Fast.ai**: Offers free deep learning courses with a hands-on approach.

These courses cater to learners at all levels, so whether you're a beginner or have some technical background, there are plenty of opportunities to grow.

1.2 Books and Research Papers

Books remain a valuable resource, especially if you want a deeper understanding of the theoretical side of AI. Here are a few to consider:

- *"Artificial Intelligence: A Guide for Thinking Humans"* by Melanie Mitchell – A great intro to the societal impacts of AI and its future.
- *"Deep Learning"* by Ian Goodfellow – A more technical dive into how deep learning works.
- *"Superintelligence: Paths, Dangers, Strategies"* by Nick Bostrom – Explores the ethical concerns surrounding advanced AI.

Research papers are also vital for staying up-to-date with the latest advancements. Websites like **arXiv.org** and **Google Scholar** provide access to thousands of academic papers on AI, helping you stay informed on cutting-edge research.

1.3 Podcasts, YouTube Channels, and Blogs

Listening to podcasts and following YouTube channels are a great way to absorb AI knowledge on the go. Here are a few popular options:

- **Lex Fridman Podcast**: In-depth interviews with experts in AI, robotics, and ethics.
- **AI Alignment Podcast**: Focuses on ensuring that AI development aligns with human values.
- **Two Minute Papers**: A YouTube channel summarizing new AI research in bite-sized videos.
- **Data Skeptic**: A podcast for those interested in machine learning, data science, and AI.

In addition to podcasts and videos, many AI-focused blogs (e.g., **OpenAI**, **DeepMind**, **Google AI Blog**) publish updates on the latest developments, breakthroughs, and trends in the field.

1.4 Industry News and Newsletters

AI is evolving rapidly, and following the latest news is crucial for understanding its real-world impact. Reputable sources include:

- **TechCrunch** and **Wired**: Cover AI developments alongside general tech news.
- **The AI Report** and **Import AI**: Newsletters dedicated entirely to AI.
- **MIT Technology Review** and **VentureBeat**: Regularly cover AI-related breakthroughs and industry shifts.

Subscribing to a mix of academic, industry-specific, and tech news outlets will give you a comprehensive view of the AI landscape.

2. Getting Involved in the AI Community

Getting engaged with the AI community can help you learn from others, exchange ideas, and stay informed. Whether you're a beginner or an expert, there are numerous ways to connect with like-minded individuals.

2.1 Join Online Communities

Online forums and discussion boards are great spaces to ask

questions, share insights, and stay updated. Here are a few popular AI communities:

- **Reddit**: Subreddits like **r/MachineLearning** and **r/ArtificialIntelligence** are active spaces where people share news, research, and resources.
- **Stack Overflow**: A go-to platform for developers seeking technical answers and solutions.
- **AI Alignment Forum**: For those interested in the ethical and future-oriented aspects of AI.

2.2 Attend AI Conferences and Meetups

Conferences are one of the best ways to network, learn about new advancements, and meet experts in the field. Some key conferences include:

- **NeurIPS** (Conference on Neural Information Processing Systems): One of the largest AI conferences, with a focus on machine learning and artificial intelligence.
- **ICML** (International Conference on Machine Learning): A premier event for machine learning researchers.
- **AI Expo and Summit**: Events that gather businesses, startups, and experts to discuss the future of AI.

If you can't attend in person, many conferences offer virtual tickets or streaming options. Local meetups on platforms like **Meetup.com** also offer informal learning and networking opportunities.

2.3 Contribute to Open Source Projects

If you have some coding skills, contributing to open-source AI projects can provide hands-on experience while enhancing your skills. Many leading AI frameworks, such as **TensorFlow**, **PyTorch**, and **OpenAI's GPT**, are open-source. Participating in these projects allows you to collaborate with others and contribute to real-world solutions.

Platforms like **GitHub** host many of these projects, providing a space for developers to contribute, share knowledge, and improve existing tools.

3. Preparing for AI's Impact on Your Career

As AI becomes a bigger part of every industry, it's important to understand its potential impact on your career. Here are a few strategies to stay relevant in an AI-driven world:

3.1 Upskilling for the Future

AI will affect nearly every industry, so it's important to upskill in areas that are becoming more crucial. Some areas to focus on include:

- **Data science and machine learning**: Learn how to work with AI tools and build models.
- **AI ethics**: Understand the ethical challenges AI presents, and how to design responsible AI systems.
- **AI product management**: If you're in business, knowledge of AI integration into products and services will be key.

3.2 Embrace AI in Your Industry

Even if you're not working directly in AI, it's essential to understand how it can be applied within your sector. From **marketing** to **healthcare**, **finance** to **education**, AI is already changing how many industries operate. Understanding AI's role can give you a competitive edge and prepare you for the future.

For instance, marketers can use AI for customer insights and personalized experiences, while healthcare professionals can leverage AI for diagnosing diseases or optimizing treatment plans.

4. Conclusion: Embrace the Future with Confidence

The future of AI is incredibly promising, and by staying informed and engaged, you can take full advantage of the opportunities it presents. Whether through continuous learning, active participation in the AI community, or preparing for AI's impact on your career, the key is to stay curious, adaptable, and proactive.

AI is not just for engineers or data scientists—it's something that will affect everyone. By understanding its capabilities and challenges, and addressing its ethical implications, we can confidently navigate this new era and ensure that AI is used for the benefit of all.

In conclusion, the AI revolution is just beginning. By embracing it thoughtfully and staying engaged, we can all contribute to a future where AI improves lives and creates new possibilities for everyone.

CONCLUSION

Artificial Intelligence (AI) has evolved from a futuristic idea to a present-day force that's already making waves in the world. Throughout this book, we've covered the basics of AI, its current and upcoming uses, and the ethical challenges it brings along. It's clear that AI has the power to transform industries, improve healthcare, tackle global issues, and open up new possibilities for innovation. But with that power comes great responsibility in how we create and use these technologies.

Looking ahead, AI offers enormous potential. But it's up to all of us—whether we're developers, policymakers, business leaders, or everyday individuals—to ensure that AI is developed and deployed thoughtfully. This means addressing critical concerns like bias, privacy, job displacement, and accountability. It also means creating a global conversation around ethical guidelines and regulations to help steer the evolution of AI in a positive direction.

If you're just starting out with AI, don't stop learning. The landscape is changing quickly, and the more we understand how AI works and what it could mean for our future, the better we can navigate its challenges and take advantage of the opportunities it brings. Whether you're looking to launch a career in AI or simply stay ahead in your current field, there are countless resources available to help you. The most important thing is to stay curious, engaged, and proactive.

In short, AI's impact is only just beginning, and we're all part of the exciting journey ahead. By approaching this technology with a sense of responsibility, awareness, and collaboration, we can shape a future where AI is a powerful force for good—improving lives and creating new opportunities across the globe.

GLOSSARY

- **AI (Artificial Intelligence)**: The ability of machines, particularly computers, to mimic human cognitive processes like learning, reasoning, problem-solving, and decision-making.
- **AGI (Artificial General Intelligence)**: A type of AI that can understand, learn, and perform tasks across a variety of domains, much like human intelligence. AGI is still theoretical and aims to match or surpass human-like thinking.
- **Algorithm**: A set of instructions or rules designed to solve a specific problem or perform a task. In AI, algorithms help machines learn from data and make decisions or predictions.
- **Bias**: Unfair or prejudiced outcomes in AI systems, typically caused by biased data or flawed assumptions during the design or training phases. This can result in unfair treatment of certain groups or individuals.
- **Deep Learning**: A subset of machine learning that uses complex neural networks with many layers to analyze large volumes of data and recognize intricate patterns.
- **Machine Learning**: A form of AI that enables machines to learn from data and improve over time, without being explicitly programmed for every task. It's the foundation for many AI applications.
- **Narrow AI**: AI that is specialized to perform a specific task, such as recognizing faces, interpreting speech, or analyzing data. It's contrasted with AGI, which would be capable of handling any intellectual task a human can do.
- **Neural Networks**: A type of algorithm inspired by the

human brain, made up of layers of interconnected nodes that process information. These are commonly used in deep learning.

- **Natural Language Processing (NLP)**: A branch of AI focused on enabling computers to understand, interpret, and generate human language, allowing for tasks like speech recognition, translation, and sentiment analysis.
- **Robotics**: The field that designs, builds, and operates robots. AI is often integrated into robots to enhance their ability to perform tasks autonomously or interact with humans.
- **Supervised Learning**: A machine learning technique where the model is trained using labeled data—data that includes both the input and the correct output—to make predictions or decisions.
- **Unsupervised Learning**: A type of machine learning where the model works with unlabeled data, finding patterns or structures without predefined categories or outcomes.
- **Training Data**: The set of data used to teach an AI model how to recognize patterns, make predictions, or solve problems. The accuracy and diversity of this data directly affect the model's performance.
- **AI Alignment**: Ensuring that AI systems behave in ways that are consistent with human values, ethics, and goals. This is especially important for more advanced systems, such as AGI, which could have far-reaching implications.
- **Automation**: The use of technology, including AI, to perform tasks that were previously done by humans. Automation can increase efficiency, reduce costs, and sometimes even replace certain types of jobs.

And that wraps up *AI for Beginners*. By now, you should have a good grasp of what artificial intelligence is, how it functions, and the incredible ways it's changing our world. As the field continues to evolve, it's important to stay curious, keep learning, and stay involved. AI is helping to shape the future, and with the right knowledge and a focus on ethics, we can harness its power to build a better, more inclusive world for all.

www.ingramcontent.com/pod-product-compliance
Lightning Source LLC
LaVergne TN
LVHW010041070326
832903LV00071B/4596